GOD GLASSES For Kids
Look What Penny Sees

Illustrations by Laura Walker
Cover Design by Marnie Ungeran
Copyright and Illustrations 2011
© by Linda Young and Ray Young
All rights reserved.

ISBN: 978-0-9841617-4-4
Published by Linda Young Ministries
Palm Desert, California

Versa Press, Inc.
1465 Spring Bay Road
East Peoria, IL 61611-9788
Printed in the United States of America
Job #J11-01044

GOD GLASSES

FOR KIDS

LOOK WHAT PENNY SEES!

by LINDA YOUNG

"Are you squeaky clean yet?"
Mom asked, as she walked
into the bathroom.
"Yep. Just like a
shiny new Penny!"
Penny giggled as she
wiggled into her pajamas.
"Okay. Be sure to brush
your teeth. I'll be in the
kitchen paying the bills.
Let me know when you're
ready and I'll tuck you in."
"Okay Mom."

Penny spit into the sink and

yelled, "M-o-m, I'm r-e-a-d-y!"

Mom put down her pen and said,

"I really need to put on

my God Glasses."

"Mom, what are God Glasses?"

Penny asked.

"They remind me to see how

God sees," Mom explained.

"They're not real. They're

invisible! I was just reminding

myself that I need to see our

money the way God sees it."

"Do God Glasses help you see everything the way God sees?" Penny asked.

"Yes." Mom said, "God sees everything through eyes of love and hope. The more you get to know God, the easier it is to see the way He sees."

"Can I have a pair of

God Glasses?"

Penny asked hopefully.

"You already have them,"

Mom smiled.

"I do?" Penny was surprised.

"Yes, Sweetheart. You do."

"The moment you asked Jesus
to be your best friend that day in
Sunday school, you had your very
own pair. All you need to do is put
them on."

"Wow. I'm going to

wear mine to bed!"

Penny said, amazed.

"There, you're all tucked in,"

Mom whispered.

"I am really tired,"

Penny said.

"Good night, Sweetheart."

"Good night, Mommy."

Penny fell asleep wearing

her God Glasses.

And she started dreaming

an amazing dream.

In Penny's dream

it was morning recess.

Everyone was outside

enjoying the sunshine.

Penny was playing hopscotch

with her friend Kayla.

Suddenly, Evan,

the new boy in school,

ran up behind Kayla and

stuck a big ooey gooey worm

right in front of her face!

Kayla did *not* like worms,

and turned to run away.

But Evan grabbed her dress

and dropped the worm

down her back.

Kayla let out a scream as the worm fell to the ground. Ugh! Everyone saw what happened and waited with mouths wide open to see what would happen next.

Penny quickly whispered,

"Kayla, put on your God Glasses."

Kayla looked at Evan and said,

"Evan, I really don't like worms,

but I do like having a new friend.

Would you like to play tag?"

That's when Evan said he was

sorry and their friendship began.

Then Penny had another dream.

Penny found herself standing

next to her teacher, Miss Harris,

who was scolding Cody Clark

for not doing his homework.

It was clear Miss Harris

was *not* happy.

Penny looked at Cody and then

back into Miss Harris' eyes.

She gently tugged on Miss Harris'

sleeve and whispered, "Miss Harris,

put on your God Glasses."

Miss Harris did not

seem to see Penny,

but her face softened

as she noticed Cody's

rumpled clothing,

unwashed hair,

and slumped shoulders.

That's when Miss Harris

remembered Cody's mom

was very sick and she realized

Cody's heart was breaking.

Miss Harris said, "Cody, would you like to have lunch with me today? I brought some homemade cookies and there are too many for me. You and I could go over your homework together." Cody looked up for the first time and smiled.

Penny had another dream.

During Miss Harris' math class,

Nathan turned his test over to see

a grade he was not expecting. F!

He said, "I am so stupid.

Why can't I do anything right?"

Penny leaned forward and whispered,

"Nathan, put on your God Glasses."

That's when Nathan stopped

saying mean things about

himself. God helped him

remember how he had read

lots of books over the summer,

all by himself. Penny smiled and

thanked God that Nathan could

see as God sees.

In Penny's next dream,

she went to Aunt Kimmie's house.

She loved playing with her cousins,

Allison, who was seven, and Anna,

who was three. Anna adored

her big sister. She wanted to do

everything that Allison did.

After snack time, Penny and
Allison ran to the playroom
leaving Anna in the kitchen,
on purpose. Being left out
made Anna mad. She stomped
into the playroom.

As Penny and Allison

began to draw pictures

of their favorite flowers,

Anna felt angry, and started

breaking the crayons!

"Stop breaking my crayons!"

Allison yelled.

But Anna just kept doing it.

Allison got very upset and

grabbed her crayons. Penny

leaned over and said, "Allison,

put on your God Glasses."

That's when Allison saw that Anna was

sad and didn't want to be left out.

Allison offered to help Anna color.

The three girls played together

drawing an entire garden!

Everyone had a great afternoon laughing and drawing pictures. Aunt Kimmie's refrigerator door never looked prettier.

"Penny, rise and shine,

breakfast is ready and

the bus will be here soon!"

"Okay Mom."

Penny walked to the bathroom.

She did not notice her

God Glasses had fallen

onto her pillow.

"Look at my hair. What a mess.

I wish my hair was as pretty

as Kayla's."

That's when Penny heard God whisper,

"Penny, put on your God Glasses."

Penny smiled.

She put on her God Glasses and

looked in the mirror again.

And then Penny heard God say,

"I really like how I made you, Penny."

Penny remembered the

dreams she had last night.

She was glad she had

her own pair of God Glasses.

"Have a fun day, Penny!"

Mom said as Penny ran to the bus.

"And Penny, don't forget to

put on your God Glasses!"

Penny smiled.

She knew it was going to be

a *very* good day.

ABOUT THE AUTHOR

Linda Young writes children's books because she wants you to know about God's never ending love. When you make Jesus your best friend, you can put on your God Glasses and see as God sees.

Turkey decided he wanted God Glasses too. Since he has been wearing them, he doesn't bark at dogs any more - well, hardly ever!

Special thanks to a ministry team
whose love for God and endless energy
made our dream a reality.

Shana Howard • Terry Lea • Brenda Nichols